So, You're in Prison?

So, you're in prison? Same routine, different day. Well, guess what? I have a way to escape prison! Maybe not in a literal sense, but a way to escape from your inner thoughts, your past regrets, and all of those things that you have been clinging to, or should I say, they are clinging to you.

The life of freedom seems like a very distant memory.

This is your life now....

Or is it?

I have a way for you to have something better than freedom from prison. Freedom, from yourself. Freedom from those lies that you have been believing, and freedom in your inner self.

What is it you may ask? Well, before I tell you, I must urge you. When I tell you, you will want to put this book down. When I tell you, you will give a huff, or a puff, and blow this book away. But again, I urge you to listen. Why might you ask? Because this may be your chance to turn it all around. Your life, yourself, and your future.

You will soon learn that, you don't have to have physical freedom, in order to be free.

Oh, I am so excited to tell you exactly what this is, but, again, I must urge you. This world has evil forces, and these evil forces will blind you. You see, there is a key. And the key that I want to share with you, those evil forces will try to blind you from it. Not in a literally, I can't see what is in front of me blind, but a spiritual force blind. Meaning that you are being blinded by something that you can't see. The blinding is done by scaling your eyes, with scales that you can not see, but you can feel them, if you reach deep down into your heart, and see this key that I am offering you.

What do I hope to get out of all of this? I hope that those scales fall off of your eyes, and that you can see what is truly in front of you.

Let me start with an explanation, before I get to the key. Are you with me? Remember, you may feel that urge to put this book down, but don't. This is those evil spiritual forces trying to get you to put this away, but, overcome that urge, and read on.

Many of you reading this, may think that this is some sort of fable. A fantasy book, one filled with stories and unrealistic tales. Well, I am about to burst that bubble of yours. This, is real. A real story, in real life. Now I know what you may be thinking. Yeah OK, this person is crazy! My response? I may sound crazy to some, but I am only crazy to the ones who are blinded by forces that they can not see.

I know, I know, why are you blinded and not me? The truth of the matter is, those forces want to blind me, but I chose this key instead. Yes, these unseen forces are against me too, and they are everywhere. But make no mistake, they are very real.

Let me ask you something, do you see the air you breath? Do you see germs? Maybe we see germs now with a microscope, but what about back then? We didn't even know that germs existed at first. How do you think that sharing this news with everyone went? Some chose to believe, and I am sure that some doubted. The ones who doubted, I wonder what they were thinking. Well, I can't see it so it's not there, I don't believe that, because that's not what we are taught, or, this can't be possible.

So here we are. Stuck between a rock and a hard place. You may already be getting doubtful, but I assure you, what I am about to tell you is real. It's as real as germs, and as real as the person reading this book. Yes, I mean you.

So, you're in prison. What if I told you, that every past failure, every regret that you have ever had, and every single mistake, could be wiped clean. What would you say? Here go your blinders, don't let your eyes make you look away, because what I am saying is true. Those evil forces are hard at work trying to keep you blinded.

Oh no, I sure hope you are still reading. Are you still there? If only I could use this page as a mirror, to see if I am talking to myself. Oh well, I guess I should keep going, hopefully someone is still reading.

So let me start by explaining these real spiritual forces, that are trying to blind you. Yes, they are still real, and no, I am not kidding. Let me start by explaining exactly what these unseen forces are.

Do you ever lay awake at night, thinking about all of your past mistakes, failures, and regrets? What if I told you, that these unseen forces, were adding to that maze of insecurities? Those negative thoughts in your head. The thoughts of inadequacy, failure, hate, etc. Now what if I told you, that you could get rid of them? Again, this is that key that I have been telling you about. But wait! I'm not ready to get there just yet.

So, these evil, unseen forces, attack you. They don't just make you think badly about yourself, but they keep you in a place of despair. The job of these forces, is to get you so down, so sad, and so depressed, that it's all you want to think about.

The job of these unseen forces, is to keep you from that key that I was telling you about. If you are focused on your sorrows, your mistakes, and your regrets, then you won't see that key, even if it's right in front of your face, which it is.

These unseen evil forces, are exactly what you would expect. They are evil, literally. Bent on your destruction, wanting you to be in not only a physical prison, but a mental one. They are dark, evil, and they play mind games. Not the fun ones either.

We are getting to the good part, are you still with me?

Have you ever seen a movie where there is a villain? The villain always tries to keep the person from being happy. Let's take Cinderella for example. These evil forces are like the stepmom who wanted Cinderella to feel terrible about herself. She wanted her working on all of these terrible tasks, ones that made her unhappy. Why did she do this? To keep her from her prince. To keep her from her key to happiness. The key that would destroy these evil forces, once and for all.

What I am about to offer you, is a key. A key that will set the captives free. Like I said, there are two types of prisons. One that is physical, and one mental. This key opens that door to your mental bondage. Those fears, regrets, and what ifs.

The reason I chose to explain these evil forces first, is so you know that once I get to that key, they will try to blind you. But, make no mistake, this key is very real.

So what's in it for me? Why am I telling you all of this? Why wouldn't I just keep this key all to myself? Do you want the simple answer of why I am going to reveal this key to you? OK, OK, here is the simple answer as to why I am about to tell you something that will change your life.

Simple answer, love.

Oh no, I said the L word, did I lose you? Hello, are you still there? Man, where is that mirror when I need it!

Well, assuming that I haven't lost you yet, I will keep going. I know, you want the answer already, but patience. It's going to come, in it's time. Don't forget, those evil forces will try and get you to turn away. By making you wait, I am showing you that you can overcome the urge of the dark forces, but you need to stay with me. Are you with me?

Those of you who have already turned away, have allowed those unseen forces to do so. But, those who are still with me, are getting prepared to hear the truth that I am about to tell you.

Some people will keep reading, some will fall off in the beginning, some in the middle, and some right before I get to the good part.

Some will also hear this key, and be blinded. Others however, those scales will fall off of your eyes, and you will see this key for what it truly is, true freedom. Not just freedom from lies, but this key holds so much more than you could ever imagine, however, I don't know if you are ready just yet. First, I have to tell you a story. This story that I am about to tell you is true, and I am not adding anything to it's account. You can choose to believe me, or you can be blinded, the choice is yours.

A long time ago, there was a man who wanted to start a war. He came against people, who had this key, the key that I have been telling you about. Again, there is no falseness to what I am about to tell you, so please, don't turn away. As you read on, those scales will hopefully start to fall off, one by one. And when you are ready, I mean really ready, I will share this key with you.

So this man, he wanted to start a war. This man, was a king, however, little did he know, that he was going against people who had this key. This was a grave mistake on his part, because he had no idea what he was in for. So every time this king tried to come against these people who had the key, he didn't succeed. The king thought that one of his own men was against him, however, one of his men let the king know, that something else was going on. You see, there was this man who knew exactly where the king was going to strike. How did he know this? Because he had the key. This mans name was Elijah. So every time the king tried to attack these people, this man Elijah, would tell the king of these people, where he was going to attack. Finding out this new information about the man, made the king angry. He wanted this man brought to him.

Are you still with me? Good, let's keep going.

OK, so we have a king who wants to destroy the king of another country. We have a man named Elijah, who has this key, telling the king where not to go, because this key allowed him to see what was up ahead, and now we have a king who is clearly upset that this man is telling the king that he is trying to destroy, how to escape him.

This story is going somewhere, so stay with me.

So the king sent his men to come and capture this man Elijah, the one who foresees where he will attack. So he sends men. The man Elijah who has been foreseeing the kings attacks, has a servant. His servant gets up early in the morning, and goes out. The servant sees that an army with horses and chariots, has surrounded the city. So the servant asked Elijah, what shall we do?

Here comes the good part! Are you ready?

Elijah then answered his servant. He told him not to be afraid, because those who are with us are more than those who are with them.

Hmm... How can there be more you might ask? Let's find out.

So the man asked the key, to open the eyes of his servant, so he could see. The servant's eyes were then opened, and he saw what you can not see with mere human eyes. What the servant saw, was that there was hills full of horses, and chariots of fire, all around them.

The servant had his eyes opened, and when they were opened, he saw that there was more fighting with them, than against them. The only thing was, that servant couldn't see at first, but once he saw, he saw that there were unseen good spiritual forces, fighting the evil forces of this world.

These are the unseen forces that I am talking about. There are good forces, and evil forces. Even though they are in the realm unseen by human eyes, the only people who are able to truly comprehend what these evil forces are, are the ones with this key.

I know, I know, this sounds like a fable, but I assure you, it's not. This is a true story.

We live in a world, where there is pain and sorrow. But, there are always evil forces who are trying to inflict as much of this pain as possible. When you have the key, you can defeat these evil forces, but only, if you have the key.

Now, do you remember when I told you that those evil forces, will try and hide this key from you? They want you blinded and kept from the truth, that there is a way out. There is a way of escape, but, you have to open your eyes to see it. There are good unseen forces, and there is a Spirit that can help your eyes be opened, but you must be aware, that those evil forces will try and keep you from this truth, because once your eyes are opened, those evil forces lose their power against you. This is why they try so hard to blind you from the truth.

Those who don't have the key, are left open to torment by these evil forces, but once you truly see this key, and accept this key, those evil forces lose their grip on you, because you no longer belong to them, but you now belong to the key. You and the key, become one.

Are the scales starting to come off yet? Are you ready to hear how to get this key? Well, I am ready to tell you, after one more story.

No! Don't put this book down! This is where some people may turn away, don't let that someone be you.

There was a man, his name was Saul. He persecuted people who had the key. He persecuted them, opposed them, put them in prison, and when they were put to death, he cast his vote against them. This man was blinded, but soon, his eyes would be opened.

This man, was so obsessed with persecuting these people who had the key, that he hunted them down. He hunted them down, even if it meant that he had to go to a foreign city to do it.

Little did he know, that on one of these journeys, his eyes would be opened.

So Saul was on one of these journeys. While he was on the road, Saul saw a light from heaven, as bright as the sun. It was blazing around him and his companions. They fell to the ground. The men who journeyed with him stood speechless, hearing a voice but seeing no one. Saul then heard a voice. The voice said these words.

Saul, Saul, why do you persecute me? It is hard for you to kick against the goads.

Saul then asked who this voice was. The voice responded that it was the key, who Saul was persecuting. The key responded with these words.

Before I tell you these words, I must warn you, this is where you will want to turn away the most. Those evil forces that I was telling you about, if you have not turned away yet, will try hard to blind you of what you are about to hear. Fight it. Let that good Spirit that I was telling you about, unblind your eyes. Let the scales fall off of your eyes, and make you see.

So the key responded with these words to Saul,

Now get up and stand on your feet. I have appeared to you to appoint you as a servant and as a witness of what you have seen and will see of me. I will rescue you from your own people and from the Gentiles. I am sending you to them to open their eyes and turn them from darkness to light, and from the power of Satan to God, so that they may receive forgiveness of sins and a place among those who are sanctified by faith in me.'

Are you still with me? Am I talking to a wall, or is someone there? Knock, knock. Is someone saying who's there? I sure hope so.

I want to share with you when Saul's scales fell off of his eyes.

The men traveling with Saul stood there speechless; they heard the sound but did not see anyone. Saul got up from the ground, but when he opened his eyes he could see nothing. So they led him by the hand into Damascus. For three days he was blind, and did not eat or drink anything.

In Damascus there was a disciple named Ananias. The Lord called to him in a vision, "Ananias!"

"Yes, Lord," he answered.

The Lord told him, "Go to the house of Judas on Straight Street and ask for a man from Tarsus named Saul, for he is praying. In a vision he has seen a man named Ananias come and place his hands on him to restore his sight."

"Lord," Ananias answered, "I have heard many reports about this man and all the harm he has done to your holy people in Jerusalem. And he has come here with authority from the chief priests to arrest all who call on your name."

But the Lord said to Ananias, "Go! This man is my chosen instrument to proclaim my name to the Gentiles and their kings and to *the people of Israel. I will show him how much he must suffer for my name."*

Then Ananias went to the house and entered it. Placing his hands on Saul, he said, "Brother Saul, the Lord—Jesus, who appeared to you on the road as you were coming here—has sent me so that you may see again and be filled with the Holy Spirit." Immediately, something like scales fell from Saul's eyes, and he could see again. He got up and was baptized, and after taking some food, he regained his strength.

Saul spent several days with the disciples in Damascus.

The key that I have been naming this whole time, this key that you will not be free without, is Jesus. These stories that I have shared, are true and come straight from the word of God. The bible tells us that people of this world are blinded by the satan, by evil forces of this world. They are blinded by the evil forces of this world who don't want you to get the key, which is Jesus. I assure you, this key is real. It's not a fable, it's not a tale, it is the only key that is true. People who turn away from this key, are blinded. But, I came to tell you that this key, Jesus, is real. I have felt His love, His presence, His forgiveness, His healing, His protection, and so much more.

You may be quick to want to put this book down, and every ounce of you may be wanting to shun it away, but I assure you, you will not be made complete without this key. You will always live in a mental bondage without it.

The crazy part is, so many people deny it, when it's free. It literally cost you nothing. Why would so many people deny a free gift? simply, because they are blinded.

So I ask you, I urge you, and I plead with you, open your eyes. The Spirit that I told you about, is the Holy Spirit. The Holy Spirit will help you see the truth.

Your past, your mistakes, and your regrets, don't affect this free gift. This man, Saul who I told you about, did things that you would assume could never be forgiven, but once his eyes were opened, he saw the truth. After this, Saul began a journey of following Jesus. A man who was once persecuting those who believed in Jesus, now set free from Jesus, and used as what Jesus Himself called, His instrument. God used a man, who once persecuted Him. God used a man, who some would have said was unforgivable, however, God forgave Him. God not only forgave him, but he used him. He gave him a purpose.

Whatever you have done, whether big or small, whatever mistakes you have made in the past, even if everyone has abandoned you, there is One that is reaching out to you, right now, in this moment. This book did not come across you by coincidence, and no this is not just some story. What I am offering you is real, and pure. Regardless of where you came from, and regardless of anything that happened before this moment, God is reaching out to you, with open arms. He is offering you forgiveness, and He is offering you a life changed. A new life in Him. The sad part is, some people will refuse this free gift, however, I hope that the Holy Spirit is guiding you into receiving this truth.

Now comes the question, how do I receive this free gift?

Before I answer this I want to tell you the why. Why would a God, who is obviously mightier than us, care about me? Why would He even care about a sinner like me? The same reason that I am writing this book.

Love. God loves you so much. You could never even imagine how much love that He has for you. Yes, you. The one reading these words. When you choose to put your faith in Jesus, He doesn't look at what you did, what you have done, or how long you have went down the wrong path, because He welcomes you with open arms. He doesn't accept you based on your past. Instead, He rejoices over you, regardless of your past, because He truly does love you.

If you are still with me, and I am hoping that you are, I am about to tell you how to receive this forgiveness, and this love. It's simple really. God doesn't ask you for money, He doesn't ask you to do all these things to be a better person before you accept Him, no, He wants you as you are. No matter how broken you feel you are, he wants you to bring yourself to Him. He wants you to come as you are. Why?

Because He wants to fix your broken pieces for you. He wants to mend your hurt, your pain, your guilt, and your sorrow. He wants you, as you are, no matter how broken you may think you are, because He loves you that much.

So, how do you have this kind of love? The bible tells us clearly how to receive it.

If you declare with your mouth, "Jesus is Lord," and believe in your heart that God raised him from the dead, you will be saved. For it is with your heart that you believe and are justified, and it is with your mouth that you profess your faith and are saved. As Scripture says, "Anyone who believes in him will never be put to shame."

Romans 10:9-11

So here you can see, all you need to do is believe. You may have heard before that Jesus died on a cross, but did you know why He died? He died so that He could save you.

He died, for love. He took the weight of all of our sins, all of our failures, all of our guilt, etc, and He hung them on the cross. He loves us so much, that He gave His life, so that you, and I, could be forgiven. If someone gave their life to save you, wouldn't that be someone who you would want to follow?

Let me explain a bit further.

We were separated from God. We were sinful, and not righteous. Jesus, came to this earth, in the form of a man, took all of our sins, and defeated them when He died on the cross. Jesus made us righteous, through His death and resurrection. And no, we didn't deserve it, but He did it anyways, because He loves us. Because Jesus did what He did for us, when you accept Jesus as your Lord and Savior, and believe in His death and resurrection, you then become forgiven. Forgiven of your sins. When this happens, God no longer looks at you and sees your past mistakes and failures, He now sees love. His love for you.

I really hope that you made it this far. I really hope that you want to follow Jesus. I have a prayer below, to help you on your journey. If you are willing to accept Jesus into your heart, please pray this with me. If you do, it will be the best decision that you will ever make.

Dear God,

I recognize that I am a sinner. I no longer want to live for the desires of this world, I want to live for you. I accept Jesus in my life, and acknowledge Him as my Lord and Savior. I believe that He died for my sins, and I believe that you rose Him from the grave on the third day. Thank you for loving me so much, that you gave your life to save mine.

In Jesus name I pray, Amen.

If you prayed that prayer, I am so proud of you! The bible tells us that when we are saved, we are now a new creation in Christ, and the old has passed away.

So from now on we regard no one from a worldly point of view. Though we once regarded Christ in this way, we do so no longer. Therefore, if anyone is in Christ, the new creation has come: The old has gone, the new is here! All this is from God, who reconciled us to himself through Christ and gave us the ministry of reconciliation

2 Corinthians 5:16-18

We are also told in the bible, that immediately once we are saved, we receive the Holy Spirit, who comes and lives inside of us.

You, however, are not in the realm of the flesh but are in the realm of the Spirit, if indeed the Spirit of God lives in you. And if anyone does not have the Spirit of Christ, they do not belong to Christ.

Romans 8:9

Therefore, if you prayed that prayer with me, and you truly meant it, then you now belong to Christ. Those spiritual forces that I mentioned in the beginning, those are real. The Holy Spirit protects you from those evil forces.

When you believed, you became sealed.

And you also were included in Christ when you heard the message of truth, the gospel of your salvation. When you believed, you were marked in him with a seal, the promised Holy Spirit,

Ephesians 1:13

From here on out, you are now part of a family of believers. You have decide to put your faith in Jesus, and for that, I rejoice. You now believe in the one who died, to set you free. Wherever you are in this moment, God sees you. If you have chosen to follow Christ, you made the best decision that you will ever make in your life. Any decisions that you have ever made that were right or wrong, this surpasses all of it. What I mean is, there is nothing bad that you have done, that this decision to follow Jesus can't overcome, and there is nothing good that you have ever done, that can surpass what you just did.

Your journey is just beginning. Are you ready?

For what I received I passed on to you as of first importance: that Christ died for our sins according to the Scriptures, that he was buried, that he was raised on the third day according to the Scriptures, and that he appeared to Cephas, and then to the Twelve. After that, he appeared to more than five hundred of the brothers and sisters at the same time, most of whom are still living, though some have fallen asleep.

1 Corinthians 15:3-8

He told them, "This is what is written: The Messiah will suffer and rise from the dead on the third day, and repentance for the forgiveness of sins will be preached in his name to all nations, beginning at Jerusalem.

Luke 24:46-47

"He himself bore our sins" in his body on the cross, so that we might die to sins and live for righteousness;

"by his wounds you have been healed."

1 Peter 2:24

When you were dead in your sins and in the uncircumcision of your flesh, God made you alive with Christ. He forgave us all our sins, having canceled the charge of our legal indebtedness, which stood against us and condemned us; he has taken it away, nailing it to the cross. And having disarmed the powers and authorities, he made a public spectacle of them, triumphing over them by the cross.

Colossians 2:13-15

While Jesus was having dinner at Matthew's house, many tax collectors and sinners came and ate with him and his disciples. When the Pharisees saw this, they asked his disciples, "Why does your teacher eat with tax collectors and sinners?"

On hearing this, Jesus said, "It is not the healthy who need a doctor, but the sick. But go and learn what this means: 'I desire mercy, not sacrifice.' For I have not come to call the righteous, but sinners."

Matthew 9:10-13

For God did not send his Son into the world to condemn the world, but to save the world through him. Whoever believes in him is not condemned, but whoever does not believe stands condemned already because they have not believed in the name of God's one and only Son.

John 3:17-18

Now the tax collectors and sinners were all gathering around to hear Jesus. But the Pharisees and the teachers of the law muttered, "This man welcomes sinners and eats with them."

Then Jesus told them this parable: "Suppose one of you has a hundred sheep and loses one of them. Doesn't he leave the ninety-nine in the open country and go after the lost sheep until he finds it? And when he finds it, he joyfully puts it on his shoulders and goes home. Then he calls his friends and neighbors together and says, 'Rejoice with me; I have found my lost sheep.' I tell you that in the same way there will be more rejoicing in heaven over one sinner who repents than over ninety-nine righteous persons who do not need to repent.

"Or suppose a woman has ten silver coins and loses one. Doesn't she light a lamp, sweep the house and search carefully until she finds it? And when she finds it, she calls her friends and neighbors together and says, 'Rejoice with me; I have found my lost coin.' In the same way, I tell you, there is rejoicing *in the presence of the angels of God over one sinner who repents."*

Jesus continued: "There was a man who had two sons. The younger one said to his father, 'Father, give me my share of the estate.' So he divided his property between them.

"Not long after that, the younger son got together all he had, set off for a distant country and there squandered his wealth in wild living. After he had spent everything, there was a severe famine in that whole country, and he began to be in need. So he went and hired himself out to a citizen of that country, who sent him to his fields to feed pigs. He longed to fill his stomach with the pods that the pigs were eating, but no one gave him anything.

"When he came to his senses, he said, 'How many of my father's hired servants have food to spare, and here I am starving to death! I will set out and go back to my father and say to him: Father, I have sinned against heaven and against you. I am no longer worthy to be called your son; make me like one of your hired servants.' So he got up and went to his father.

"But while he was still a long way off, his father saw him and was filled with compassion for him; he ran to his son, threw his arms around him and kissed him.

"The son said to him, 'Father, I have sinned against heaven and against you. I am no longer worthy to be called your son.'

"But the father said to his servants, 'Quick! Bring the best robe and put it on him. Put a ring on his finger and sandals on his feet. Bring the fattened calf and kill it. Let's have a feast and celebrate. For this son of mine was dead and is alive again; he was lost and is found.' So they began to celebrate.

"Meanwhile, the older son was in the field. When he came near the house, he heard music and dancing. So he called one of the servants and asked him what was going on. 'Your brother has come,' he replied, 'and your father has killed the fattened calf because he has him back safe and sound.'

"The older brother became angry and refused to go in. So his father went out and pleaded with him. But he answered his father, 'Look! All these years I've been slaving for you and never disobeyed your orders. Yet you never gave me even a young goat so I could celebrate with my friends. But when this son of yours who has squandered your property with prostitutes comes home, you kill the fattened calf for him!'

"'My son,' the father said, 'you are always with me, and everything I have is yours. But we had to celebrate and be glad, because

this brother of yours was dead and is alive
again; he was lost and is found.'"

Luke 15

God rejoices, when the lost are found.

To see more books or study guides by
Tentmaker Ministries, please visit
Tm-Ministries.com

Printed in Great Britain
by Amazon

47223796R10030